For my mother
—A.H.

For Grandpa, Mom, and Marie
—L.D.G.

Random House ⌂ New York

Text copyright © 1997 by Alice Herck.
Illustrations copyright © 1997 by Linda Dockey Graves.
All rights reserved under International and Pan-American Copyright Conventions.
Published in the United States by Random House, Inc., New York,
and simultaneously in Canada by Random House of Canada Limited, Toronto.

http://www.randomhouse.com/

Library of Congress Cataloging-in-Publication Data:
Herck, Alice. The enchanted gardening book : ideas for using plants
to beautify your world, both indoors and out / by Alice Herck ;
illustrated by Linda Dockey Graves.   p.   cm.
SUMMARY: A step-by-step guide to creative gardening,
with ideas from a delicate doll's garden to a tropical rainforest.
ISBN: 0-679-88096-8 (trade)   1. Gardening—Juvenile literature.
2. Nature craft—Juvenile literature.   [1. Gardening.   2. Nature Craft.   3. Handicraft.]
I. Graves, Linda, ill.   II. Title.   SB457.H46   1997   635.9—dc20   96–31704
Printed in the United States of America

10 9 8 7 6 5 4 3 2 1

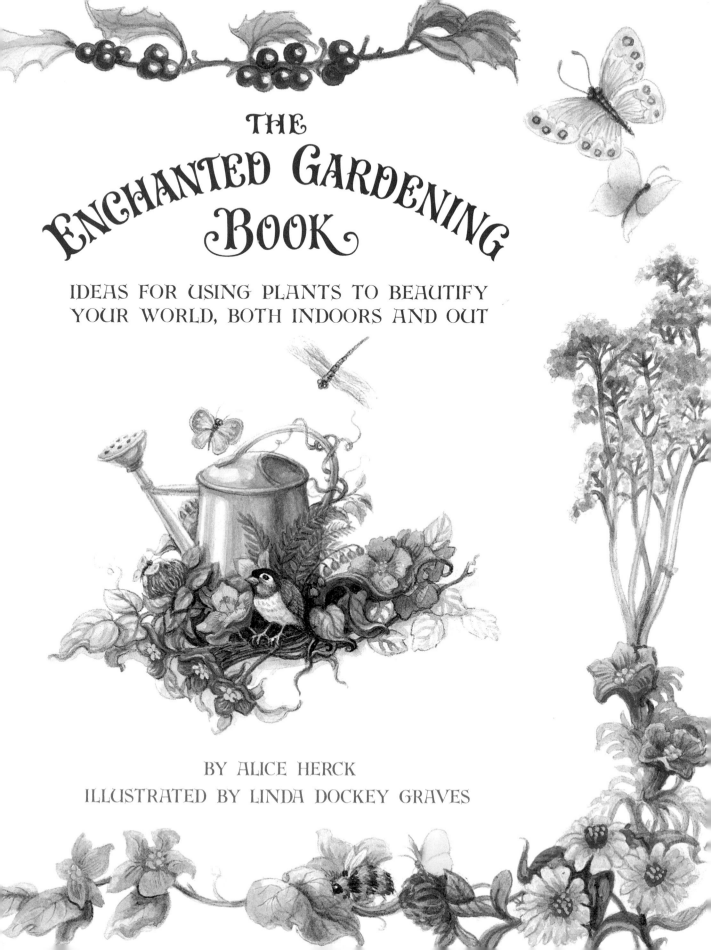

THE ENCHANTED GARDENING BOOK

IDEAS FOR USING PLANTS TO BEAUTIFY YOUR WORLD, BOTH INDOORS AND OUT

BY ALICE HERCK

ILLUSTRATED BY LINDA DOCKEY GRAVES

Dear Reader:

Of all the hobbies in the world, gardening is the most rewarding because it gives you so much for practically nothing.

Gardening is enchanted. Stems, leaves, flowers, herbs, and trees seem to rise magically from the dirt to transform a space. A yard becomes a garden filled with butterflies. An empty lot changes into a fairyland. A window turns into a leafy frame for the world. A terra-cotta pot changes into a doll's garden.

But the most important magic gardening brings is that it lets *you* change the future of the natural world! By pulling out weeds around a seedling, you help it grow into a tree, so that your yard or park or city street remains a good place for future generations of wildlife and people to live.

Not only that, gardening is inexpensive and easy. For less than the price of a jumbo candy bar, you can buy a three-inch pot containing practically *any* houseplant you wish to grow. And if you can follow the directions on a box of cake mix, you can grow a plant.

Plant a seed or tend a plant—that's the way to let enchantment blossom!

Alice Herk

CONTENTS

BEGINNERS' BASICS

Garden centers are stores that sell plants, seeds, soil, and other gardening supplies. Check in the Yellow Pages for one nearby. You can also find the names and addresses of mail-order garden supply stores in many adult gardening books in your public library.

It's tempting to buy seed packets. But it's much *easier*, and often no more expensive, to buy small plants called seedlings or transplants and put them into your garden or containers. Houseplant transplants are available year round at garden centers. Transplants that are commonly grown outdoors, such as flowers, herbs, and trees, are more available in spring and summer. Look carefully at plants before you buy them. Avoid ones with brown or sick-looking leaves, insects, or roots hanging out. Buy flowering plants with unopened buds.

Most plants come with tags explaining the care they need. If you find one that doesn't come with instructions, see if any are available. Garden centers want the plants they sell to grow—otherwise you won't come back and buy more! So feel free to ask about any plant you want to buy.

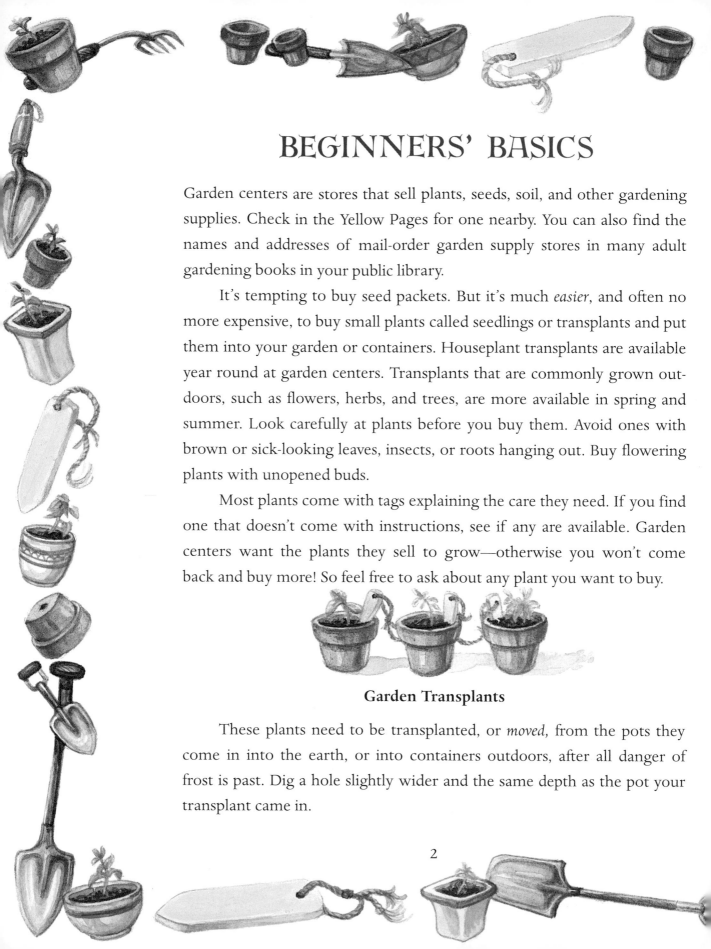

Garden Transplants

These plants need to be transplanted, or *moved,* from the pots they come in into the earth, or into containers outdoors, after all danger of frost is past. Dig a hole slightly wider and the same depth as the pot your transplant came in.

ᔑ To remove the transplant from its pot, hold one hand flat over the surface of the soil, with the stem of the plant between your fingers. Turn the pot over. If the transplant doesn't slide right out, *gently* pull at it while tapping the base of the pot. Set the plant in the hole and fill around it with soil. Gently press on the soil around the plant with your hands. Water thoroughly. If the soil washes away in places and pockets of air form, add more soil. Then water and add more soil until the pockets disappear.

Container Transplants

Containers for growing plants vary. You can use clay or plastic pots, wooden half-barrels, concrete cinder blocks, even old teapots! They all need a hole in the bottom to let water drain out. You'll also need a saucer, cookie sheet, or bowl underneath to catch the draining water.

Put a shallow layer of potting soil (special sterilized dirt available at all garden centers) in your container. To check the depth, set your transplant, *still in its plastic pot,* inside the container. Put your transplant aside and add or remove enough potting soil so that the top of the plastic pot rests about one inch below the top of the container. Follow from the ᔑ in Garden Transplants.

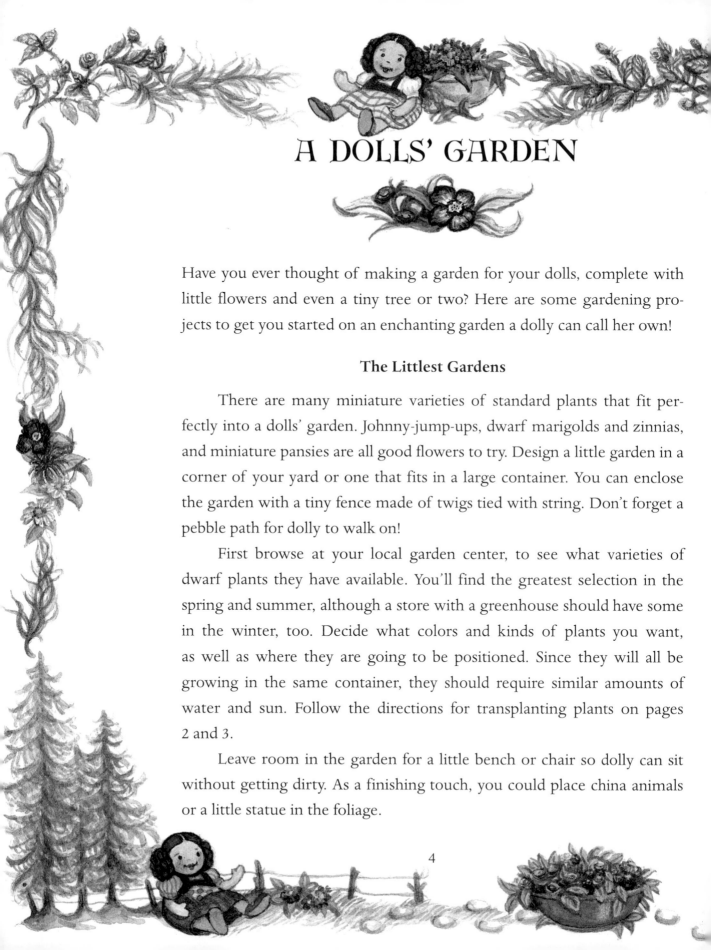

A DOLLS' GARDEN

Have you ever thought of making a garden for your dolls, complete with little flowers and even a tiny tree or two? Here are some gardening projects to get you started on an enchanting garden a dolly can call her own!

The Littlest Gardens

There are many miniature varieties of standard plants that fit perfectly into a dolls' garden. Johnny-jump-ups, dwarf marigolds and zinnias, and miniature pansies are all good flowers to try. Design a little garden in a corner of your yard or one that fits in a large container. You can enclose the garden with a tiny fence made of twigs tied with string. Don't forget a pebble path for dolly to walk on!

First browse at your local garden center, to see what varieties of dwarf plants they have available. You'll find the greatest selection in the spring and summer, although a store with a greenhouse should have some in the winter, too. Decide what colors and kinds of plants you want, as well as where they are going to be positioned. Since they will all be growing in the same container, they should require similar amounts of water and sun. Follow the directions for transplanting plants on pages 2 and 3.

Leave room in the garden for a little bench or chair so dolly can sit without getting dirty. As a finishing touch, you could place china animals or a little statue in the foliage.

Dolls' Rose Wall

Topped with doll-size roses, this "brick wall" can be part of an indoor or outdoor dolls' garden, enjoyed alone, or placed beside other potted miniature plants or flowers. Try this gardening project with different kinds of miniature flowers as well.

You will need:

A rectangular terra-cotta planter, at least 6″ deep, with drainage holes, and something to use as a saucer

Pot shards (several pieces of broken clay pottery)

Potting soil

Enough miniature rose transplants to fill your planter (available at most garden centers)

1) If you're doing this project inside, put a large plastic garbage bag over your work surface to protect it and keep it clean.

2) Position pot shards over the drainage holes in the planter.

3) Cover the bottom of the planter with a shallow layer of soil.

4) Decide the order in which you want the roses to grow. Line them up in their plastic pots and try rearranging them. Make sure you're pleased with how they look before moving to the next step.

5) Follow the directions on pages 2 and 3 for transplanting your roses. Add just as much soil as necessary to hold the plants in place. Work as quickly as possible.

UPKEEP: Place your rose wall in a sunny window. In warm weather you can take it outdoors. Follow the watering instructions that come with your roses.

Fanciful Forests

You can make a doll-size forest grove by arranging small potted evergreens together. A forest of potted dwarf palm trees or tiny cacti will make a doll feel as if she's in a tropical paradise!

For a perfect little tree, buy or grow a rosemary or bay standard. Standards are plants trained over a long period of time to grow like trees. They tend to be slightly expensive and are available in fancier garden centers.

MINIATURE RAINFOREST

You can have a little rainforest by making a terrarium. Lightly water a terrarium when it's first planted, and you may never need to water again! Plants' roots absorb water, and their leaves release a fine water vapor. The vapor is trapped inside the covered terrarium and turns to water. The water drips down the glass, into the soil, and the cycle begins all over.

Terrarium Plants

A terrarium plant should like moisture, be slow-growing, and have needs similar to those of other plants it will be growing with.

If you are using wild plants, prepare your terrarium first, as they need to be transplanted as soon as possible. Fall is the best season for gathering wild plants such as ferns, mosses, seedling trees, and evergreens.

If you are buying plants, try small African violets, Christmas cactus, crotons, dwarf palms, English ivy, spider or zebra plants. Don't worry about choosing the wrong plants. Some will flourish. Some will not. Enjoy the show.

Terrarium

You will need:

Aquarium gravel	*2 or 3 crumbled charcoal briquettes*
Potting soil	*Clean glass fishtank or bowl*
Rocks and/or tree branches	*Variety of plants (see above)*
Plastic wrap	*Spray bottle with water*

8

1) Place 1 to 2 inches of gravel mixed with crumbled charcoal in the bottom of a fishtank. Add double that amount of potting soil.

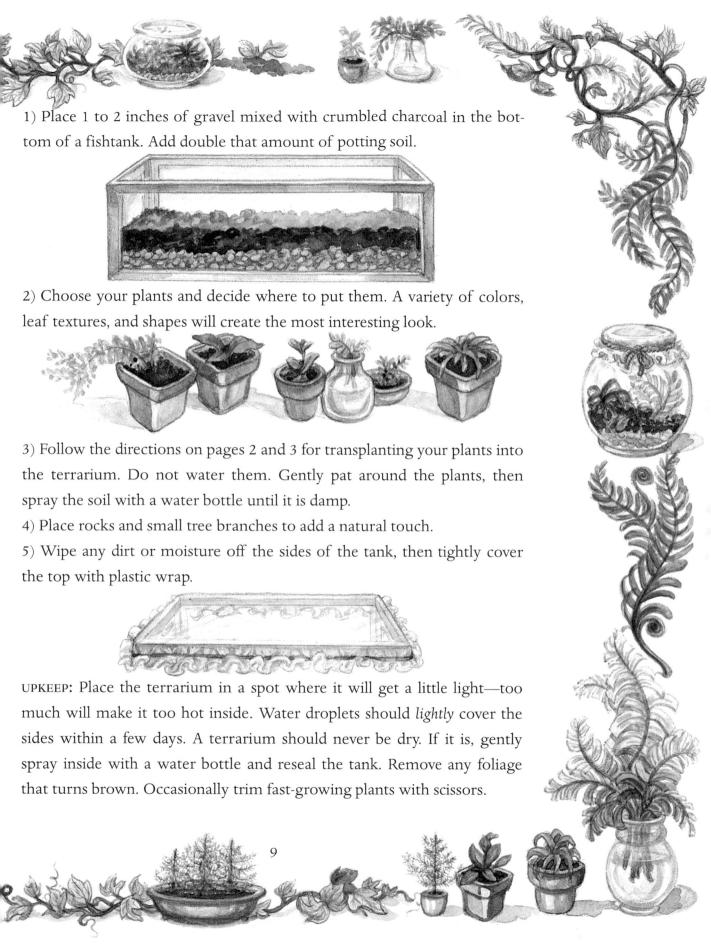

2) Choose your plants and decide where to put them. A variety of colors, leaf textures, and shapes will create the most interesting look.

3) Follow the directions on pages 2 and 3 for transplanting your plants into the terrarium. Do not water them. Gently pat around the plants, then spray the soil with a water bottle until it is damp.

4) Place rocks and small tree branches to add a natural touch.

5) Wipe any dirt or moisture off the sides of the tank, then tightly cover the top with plastic wrap.

UPKEEP: Place the terrarium in a spot where it will get a little light—too much will make it too hot inside. Water droplets should *lightly* cover the sides within a few days. A terrarium should never be dry. If it is, gently spray inside with a water bottle and reseal the tank. Remove any foliage that turns brown. Occasionally trim fast-growing plants with scissors.

9

A ROSE IS A ROSE

In the fairy tale *Beauty and the Beast,* the only gift Beauty wanted was a single red rose. Start your own fairy-tale rose garden, buy a bunch of roses, or give a rose to your favorite person—and live happily ever after!

Rose Land

Roses are a real challenge to grow. They need lots of sun, rich soil, and good drainage, as well as love and care, in order to thrive. There are many books about growing and caring for roses. Read a few before starting a garden. Floribunda and polyantha roses are generally the easiest kinds to grow, but ask at a garden center for the right plant for your local conditions. For an indoor rose garden, try the "Rose Wall" on page 6.

If growing and caring for roses is too big an undertaking, store-bought roses can be almost as fulfilling. Help your roses last longer by putting them in a vase filled with water and a teaspoon of sugar. With an adult's help, trim the stems every other day, cutting them diagonally. You can sometimes revive drooping roses by immersing them in a sinkful of cool water for an hour or so.

Forever Roses

Picked roses last only a week or so. But if you dry them, you'll have them forever. Follow the directions for drying flowers on page 16. Try arranging different colors and kinds of dried roses in a vase or tuck them into a wreath like the one on page 18.

Rose Beads

A dozen fresh roses will make 15 to 20 marble-size beads. Pull the petals off the flowers and mash them with a mortar and pestle, or in a glass bowl with a wooden spoon. Spread the mashed petals—which will look like chopped spinach—on waxed paper, then let them dry for an hour.

Put the dried mashed petals back into the bowl and mash them again. Continue drying and mashing the petals until you have a fine paste. Add drops of water as needed.

Dab your fingertips in rose-scented oil. Squeeze the paste into little balls, about the size of marbles. Place the balls on clean waxed paper and allow them to dry for an hour. Then, with an adult's help, carefully poke a hole through each ball with a thick sewing needle. Allow the beads to dry for several days on the waxed paper.

Make a necklace by stringing the rose beads on nylon fishing line.

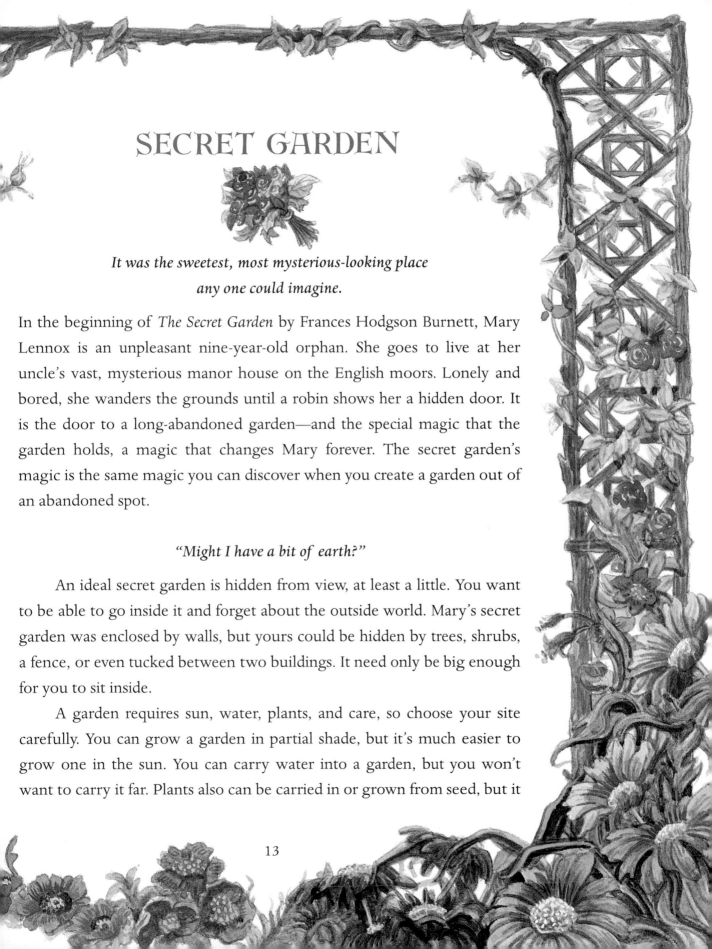

SECRET GARDEN

*It was the sweetest, most mysterious-looking place
any one could imagine.*

In the beginning of *The Secret Garden* by Frances Hodgson Burnett, Mary Lennox is an unpleasant nine-year-old orphan. She goes to live at her uncle's vast, mysterious manor house on the English moors. Lonely and bored, she wanders the grounds until a robin shows her a hidden door. It is the door to a long-abandoned garden—and the special magic that the garden holds, a magic that changes Mary forever. The secret garden's magic is the same magic you can discover when you create a garden out of an abandoned spot.

"Might I have a bit of earth?"

An ideal secret garden is hidden from view, at least a little. You want to be able to go inside it and forget about the outside world. Mary's secret garden was enclosed by walls, but yours could be hidden by trees, shrubs, a fence, or even tucked between two buildings. It need only be big enough for you to sit inside.

A garden requires sun, water, plants, and care, so choose your site carefully. You can grow a garden in partial shade, but it's much easier to grow one in the sun. You can carry water into a garden, but you won't want to carry it far. Plants also can be carried in or grown from seed, but it is easier to make a garden if there are already some plants growing. Care, of course, is provided by you. Keep it simple.

The grass seemed so thick
in some of the places where the green points
were pushing their way through that she thought
they did not seem to have room enough to grow.

After you've cleaned up any litter in your chosen spot, it's time to give the plants already there room to grow. This is called weeding. Mary weeded her secret garden without knowing anything about gardening. Weeding is easiest to do the day after a soaking rain. For tight spots and tough weeds, use your hands or a dandelion fork. A hoe is handy for larger areas.

"It wouldn't seem like a secret garden if it was tidy."

Grow a garden as wild as your imagination! Blur the edges with evergreens and shrubs. Plant climbing vines to creep up trees and walls and fences. Select tall flowers suited to your site and plant them around the outside of the garden. Grow shorter ones inside, where they will be your secret treasures. Fill every nook and cranny with some glorious green living thing!

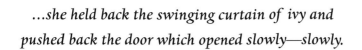

*…she held back the swinging curtain of ivy and
pushed back the door which opened slowly—slowly.*

The way we enter a garden affects our experience inside. An archway of climbing vines is inviting, beautiful, and quite easy to create. Make a simple arch by pounding two tall, heavy stakes into the ground and stringing a piece of wire between them at the top. Plant ivy at the base of each stake, and train its vines to grow up and around by loosely attaching them to the stakes with plastic-coated twist ties.

Try adding a romantic touch or two to your garden. You can paint a bench gold or put up a picket fence. Easy-to-install pieces of white or unpainted picket fence are available at most garden centers. You can also find great inexpensive ceramic containers and statuary at garage sales.

"Even if it isn't real Magic…something is there—something!"

The most important and fun thing to do inside any secret garden is to experience the magic in it. Exactly what that is is hard to say. Certainly it is a good thing, more easily felt than described.

Smell the rich, warm earth, listen to the wind, and touch the plants each day. Something is there. Something. You will feel it too, just as Mary Lennox did.

EVERLASTING SUMMER

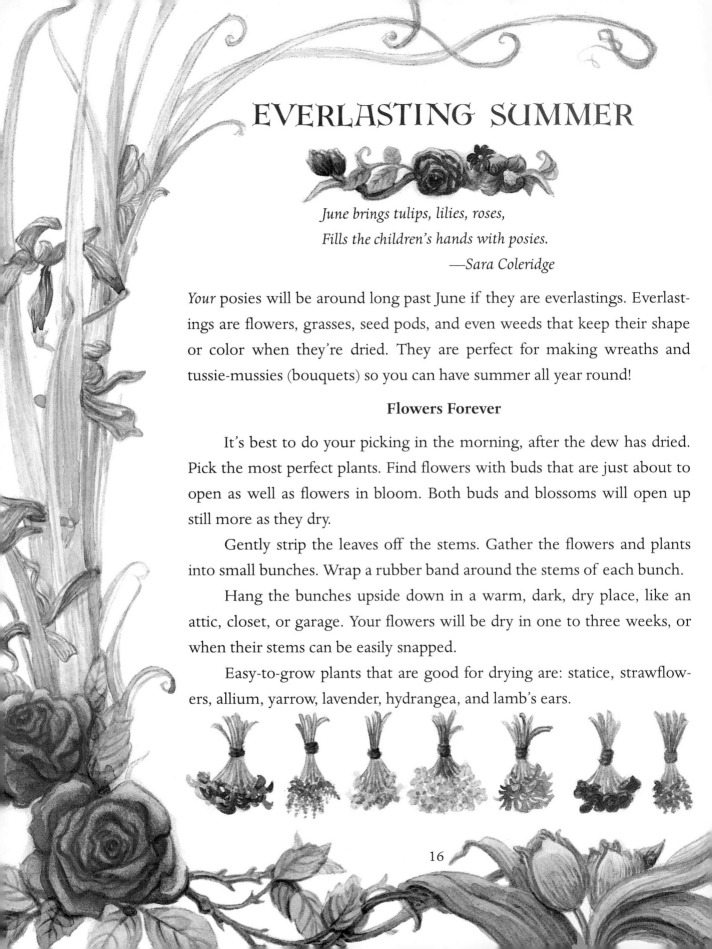

June brings tulips, lilies, roses,
Fills the children's hands with posies.
—Sara Coleridge

Your posies will be around long past June if they are everlastings. Everlastings are flowers, grasses, seed pods, and even weeds that keep their shape or color when they're dried. They are perfect for making wreaths and tussie-mussies (bouquets) so you can have summer all year round!

Flowers Forever

It's best to do your picking in the morning, after the dew has dried. Pick the most perfect plants. Find flowers with buds that are just about to open as well as flowers in bloom. Both buds and blossoms will open up still more as they dry.

Gently strip the leaves off the stems. Gather the flowers and plants into small bunches. Wrap a rubber band around the stems of each bunch.

Hang the bunches upside down in a warm, dark, dry place, like an attic, closet, or garage. Your flowers will be dry in one to three weeks, or when their stems can be easily snapped.

Easy-to-grow plants that are good for drying are: statice, strawflowers, allium, yarrow, lavender, hydrangea, and lamb's ears.

16

Summer Wreath

Buy a plain grapevine wreath from a craft store or make one by wrapping grape or ivy vines into a circle. Hold the vines in place with thin string. Attach a loop of wire to the back of the wreath for hanging.

With an adult's help, use a hot glue gun to attach statice flowers to the wreath base. Let the wreath dry for two hours. Glue individual strawflower blossoms on and around the statice. Allow the wreath to dry on a flat surface overnight. For a final touch, add ribbons or bows to your finished wreath.

Tussie-mussies

Tussie-mussies are little bouquets of fragrant flowers and herbs. In Victorian England, people made these tiny nosegays to send messages to each other. Make a tussie-mussie and send it to someone special.

Select a fresh or dried flower that expresses the main message you'd like to send. Use roses for love, green ivy for friendship, mint for virtue, and zinnias for missing someone. Surround that flower with other blooms or herbs that express the rest of your message. Tie a rubber band around the stems to form a bunch.

Cut an X in the center of a doily, then gently push the flower stems through the X. Tie a ribbon around the stems, just under the paper doily.

Perhaps there are other "feelings," or flowers, you would like to include in your tussie-mussie. Make up some flower meanings of your own. Just be sure to include a note to let the person know what the flowers stand for!

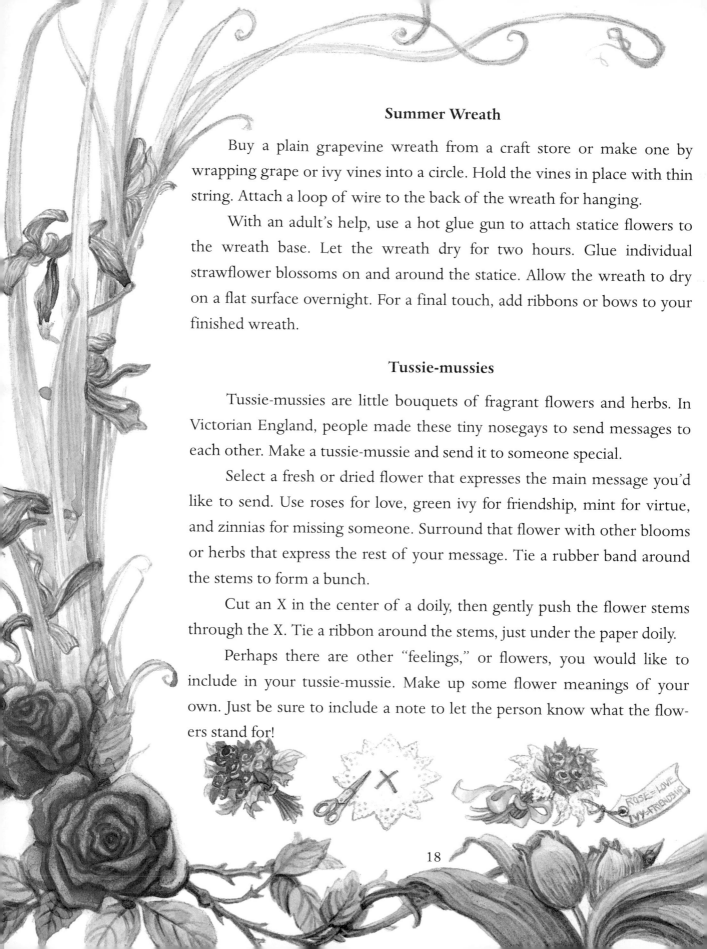

18

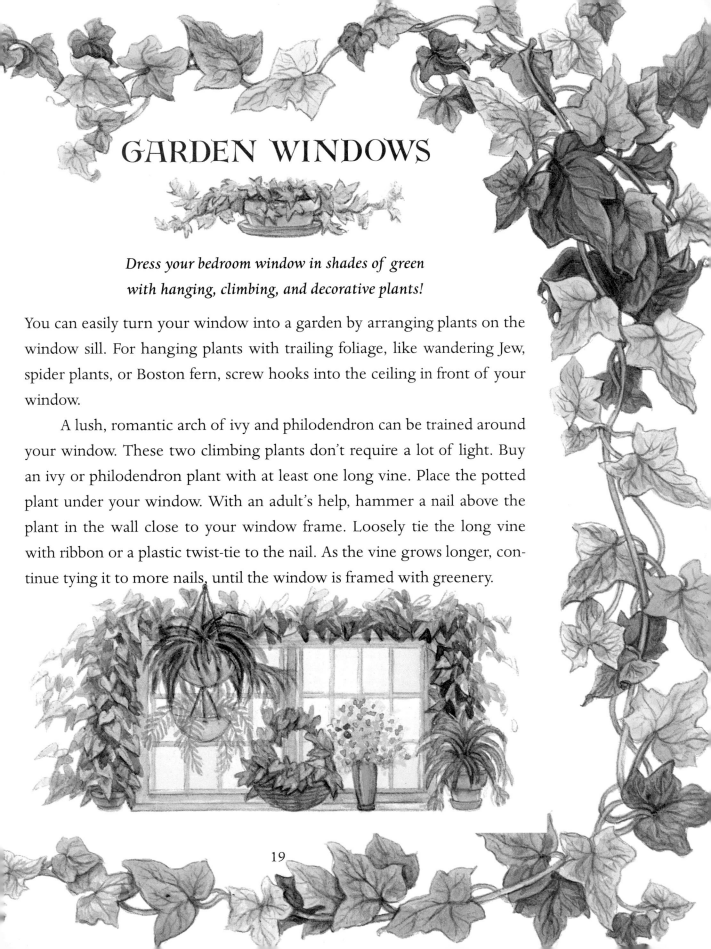

GARDEN WINDOWS

*Dress your bedroom window in shades of green
with hanging, climbing, and decorative plants!*

You can easily turn your window into a garden by arranging plants on the window sill. For hanging plants with trailing foliage, like wandering Jew, spider plants, or Boston fern, screw hooks into the ceiling in front of your window.

A lush, romantic arch of ivy and philodendron can be trained around your window. These two climbing plants don't require a lot of light. Buy an ivy or philodendron plant with at least one long vine. Place the potted plant under your window. With an adult's help, hammer a nail above the plant in the wall close to your window frame. Loosely tie the long vine with ribbon or a plastic twist-tie to the nail. As the vine grows longer, continue tying it to more nails, until the window is framed with greenery.

BUTTERFLY AND BIRD GARDEN

Hurt no living thing;
Ladybird, nor butterfly,
Nor moth with dusty wing…
—*Christina Rossetti*

Did you ever want a butterfly to float down and land in the palm of your hand? You can enchant butterflies and birds simply by planting their favorite flowers in your backyard or terrace.

Once these fluttering beauties have winged their way to you, they will actually help your garden grow. Butterflies pollinate flowers, making them produce seeds. Seeds grow into new plants, which flower and attract *more* butterflies! Birds eat the insects so the insects can't eat your plants. Did you know that a single swallow can swallow more than 1,000 flying insects in 12 hours?

Plant some of these tried-and-true, butterfly-and-bird-pleasing plants in your garden and watch what happens!

Zinnias, Marigolds, and More

Brightly colored marigolds and zinnias are very easy to start from seeds. In the spring, after the soil is warm, plant the seeds in full sun, directly in the garden or in containers, following the instructions on the seed packet. Water the full-grown plants when the soil is dry. Cut back the flowers after they bloom in order to encourage new growth.

Other good plants for attracting nectar-sipping butterflies include: butterfly weed, butterfly bush, petunias, phlox, daisies, and cosmos. Or look up a specific butterfly's favorite flowers in a field guide and try planting some in your yard.

Parsley Nursery

Another way you can bring butterflies to your garden is to plant parsley. Why? Because swallowtail butterflies like to lay their eggs on parsley plants!

Each butterfly starts life as an egg, which hatches into a caterpillar. The baby caterpillar eats the leaves of the parsley plant. Then, when it has eaten enough, the caterpillar spins a chrysalis. Inside the chrysalis, the caterpillar grows and changes. When it hatches, out comes a beautiful butterfly!

In the early spring, buy several parsley plants at a nursery. (That way, you'll have enough for the butterflies *and* for you to add some to summer salads.) Plant the parsley in full sun, directly in the garden or in containers.

Bountiful Bee Balm

The shaggy red, pink, or white flowers of bee balm will entice butterflies, bees, and even hummingbirds to visit you! In the spring, after the soil has warmed, transplant bee balm plants into the garden or a large container in full or partial sun. Keep the soil moist.

After blooming, cut the plants back nearly to the ground to encourage new growth. Bee balm is a perennial plant that spreads easily and will come back year after year!

Birds' Banquet

A yard with a wide variety of trees, shrubs, and flowers will always attract a bevy of birds.

To ensure a plentiful food supply, plant fruit- and nut-bearing trees and shrubs that are native to your area. Evergreen trees, like cedar or spruce, are also important, as they provide cover in winter, when fruit- and nut-bearing trees drop their leaves.

If you don't have a yard, or want to attract birds quickly, you can scatter birdseed on the ground or hang a feeder from a tree or pole.

No Pesticides, Please!

Pesticides may kill harmful insect pests. But they also harm the pests' natural enemies. If you want to attract birds and butterflies to your yard, don't use pesticides.

Seeds on a Silver Platter

You will need:

 1 8" x 8" x 2" aluminum baking pan

 Hammer and nail

 4 3-foot-long pieces of wire

1) Get an adult to help you punch ten small holes in the bottom of an aluminum pan using a hammer and nail. This will allow rainwater to drain from the feeder.

2) Hammer a nail hole into each of the four upper corners of the pan.

3) Slide a wire into each of the upper corner holes. Twist the loose ends together, leaving room at the top to twist or tie them around a tree branch or pole.

4) Pour an inch of birdseed into the pan.

5) Watch the birds come in for a landing!

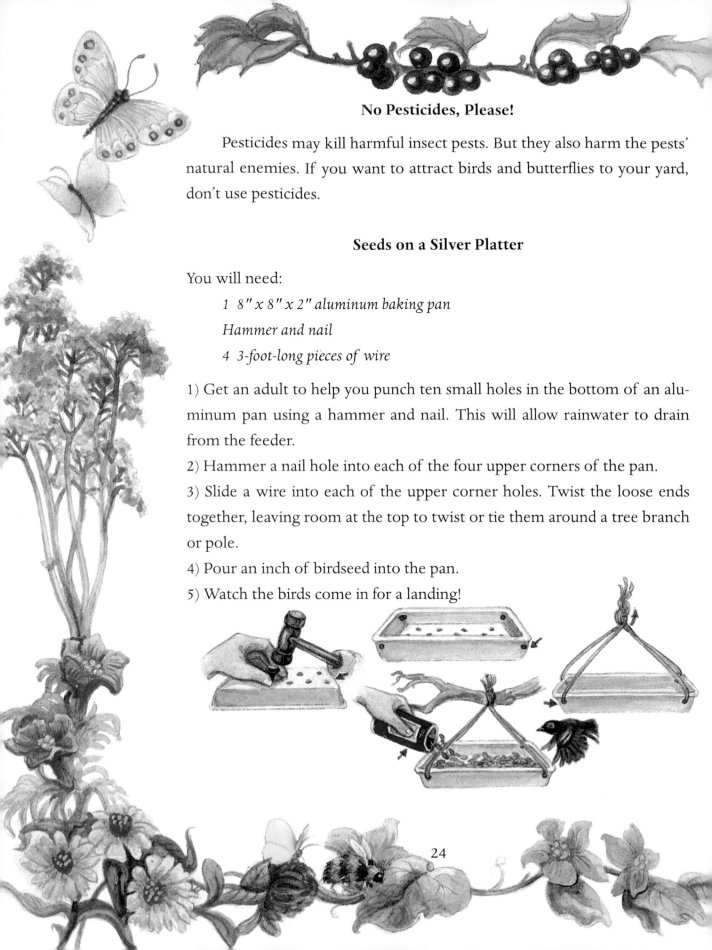

Extra-Easy Bird Feeders

🐦 Slather pine cones with peanut butter, then roll them in birdseed and hang them from a tree or on a hook outside a window.

🐦 Fill a plastic mesh bag with stale bread and hang it outside.

🐦 Wedge pieces of apple, orange, or banana between tree branches.

Bathing Beauties

You can buy a birdbath or make one from a shallow pan or bowl. In either case, it needs to be at least three feet off the ground, and not contain more than three inches of water. Tree stumps, rocks, and bricks make good platforms.

Place the bath in the open, near a tree or shrub. This way, bathing birds can see a hungry kitty and make a quick getaway!

Bell That Cat!

Cats are hunters by nature and can't help wanting to catch birds. So if you have a cat, it's a good idea to put a bell on its collar.

MAGICAL MINT

The cool, clean smell of mint makes you feel refreshed and invigorated. What's the magical ingredient? It's *menthol*, which stimulates the cells in our skin that are affected by the cold.

Sprigs of mint make a great garnish and add a zesty flavor to ice water. Add chopped mint to ice cream or yogurt.

Plant a mini mint garden and create a little mint magic of your own!

Mini Mint Garden

You will need:

1 large bag potting soil

1 clay pot big enough to stand 2 or 3 coffee cans inside

2 or 3 coffee cans with the tops and bottoms removed

2 or 3 mint plants (such as peppermint, spearmint, or apple mint)

1) Place a layer of potting soil in the clay pot. Stand the coffee cans in the pot on top of the soil. (The top of the cans should reach about 1 inch below the top of the pot.)

2) Add more soil to the pot, filling in and around the cans. If the soil is very dry, water it lightly. You should barely see the tops of the cans.

3) Dig a hole in each can for a mint plant.

4) Take the mints out of their containers and place them in the holes. Gently press the plants in place. Add extra soil, if needed.

5) Water the pot until the soil is completely wet and water drains from the

bottom. If soil washes away, forming empty pockets, add more soil. Water and add more soil until the pockets are gone.

6) Mint will grow best in partial shade. Place your mini mint garden inside near a sunny window.

UPKEEP: In warm weather, take your mint plants outdoors. Keep the soil moist. Snip off fresh mint leaves as you need them. You can also dry mint by hanging it in loose bunches upside down in a dark, dry place like a closet.

Roman Bath and Sachet

For a mint-scented bath, get an adult to help you simmer 1 cup of mint leaves in a quart of water. After 20 minutes, strain and pour the mint water into the full bathtub. Place the wet mint leaves in the center of a washcloth and tie it up with a ribbon. Soak in the tub, and rub the washcloth on your arms and legs. You'll feel magically rested and revived!

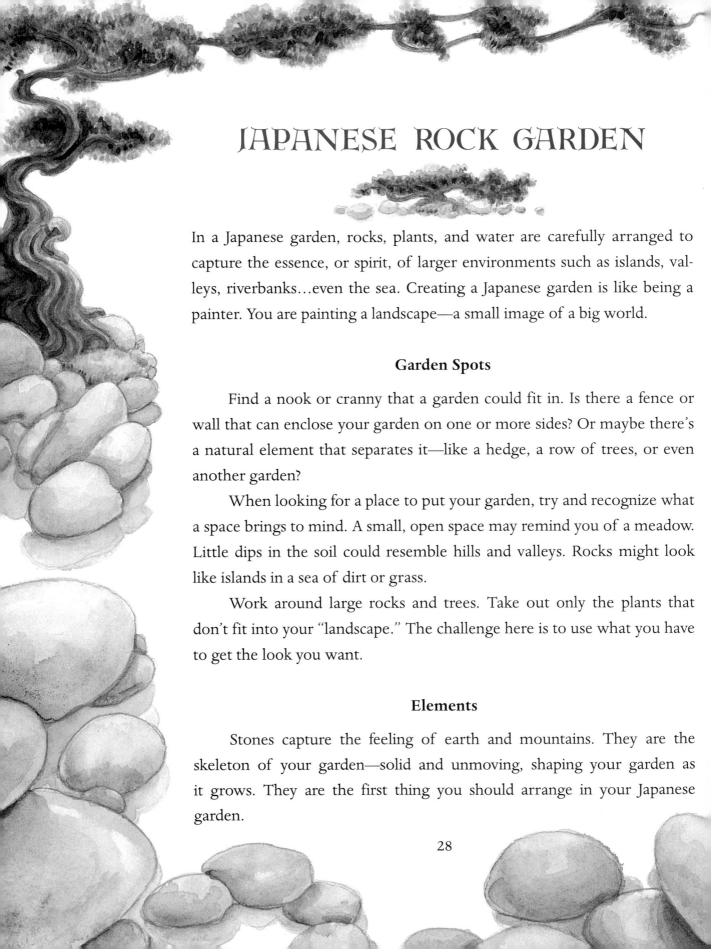

JAPANESE ROCK GARDEN

In a Japanese garden, rocks, plants, and water are carefully arranged to capture the essence, or spirit, of larger environments such as islands, valleys, riverbanks…even the sea. Creating a Japanese garden is like being a painter. You are painting a landscape—a small image of a big world.

Garden Spots

Find a nook or cranny that a garden could fit in. Is there a fence or wall that can enclose your garden on one or more sides? Or maybe there's a natural element that separates it—like a hedge, a row of trees, or even another garden?

When looking for a place to put your garden, try and recognize what a space brings to mind. A small, open space may remind you of a meadow. Little dips in the soil could resemble hills and valleys. Rocks might look like islands in a sea of dirt or grass.

Work around large rocks and trees. Take out only the plants that don't fit into your "landscape." The challenge here is to use what you have to get the look you want.

Elements

Stones capture the feeling of earth and mountains. They are the skeleton of your garden—solid and unmoving, shaping your garden as it grows. They are the first thing you should arrange in your Japanese garden.

28

Find stones of different shapes and colors. As any gardener will confirm, you'll find many rocks already *in* your garden! You can also buy smooth tumbled stones that come in an array of colors and look very special if used sparingly. Arrange the stones in a manner that fits in with your "landscape."

You needn't install a fishpond to have water in your garden. A birdbath or weathered washbasin will do nicely. To *suggest* the presence of water, consider adding a raked gravel area to the garden, or using stones and pebbles to make a dry streambed.

Plants

Japanese gardens rely on the subtle shades of evergreen trees and shrubs, ferns, bamboo, and other grasses to create a year-round soothing effect. Plant your greenery in an arrangement that pleases *your* eye.

Evergreen plants are perhaps the most important element in a Japanese garden. Ask at a garden center for varieties of evergreens and ferns that are suited to your area. Evergreens are best planted in the spring or fall. Ferns grow well in moist shade and create great woodland scenes.

Bamboo is common in Japanese gardens. However, it does not grow naturally in every location. There are two kinds of bamboo plants—the kind that spreads rapidly via runners and the kind that grows slowly in clumps. Stick to the clumping kind if you are planting directly into the earth. Or plant bamboo in a large container—black bamboo is a good choice. Make sure any bamboo plant you buy comes with growing instructions.

Choose flowering trees and shrubs for seasonal color. Aim to have only one or two plants flowering during each season. Perennial flowers and flowering trees and shrubs are all good choices.

Human Nature

Most importantly, place one or two well-worn, man-made objects in your garden. Scour garage sales for old basins, teapots, or lanterns. Putting man-made items in your garden will remind you that people are as much a piece of the natural world as plants, rocks, and water—part of the ancient and constant mystery of life.

FLOWER POWER

The golden crocus reaches up
To catch a sunbeam in her cup.
> —Walter Crane

It's snowing outside. Your front walk is caked with ice. The rosebushes are buried beneath six feet of snow. What you need are sights and smells of spring!

If you learn how to "force" bulbs to grow, you will have the "flower power" to bring on spring at any time of the year. There are two kinds of bulbs that you can grow indoors by "forcing." One kind you simply plant and water. The other kind must be refrigerated before planting. You can buy both plain and pre-chilled bulbs at most garden centers.

Paper-whites

You will need:

1 shallow waterproof bowl
Gravel or pebbles
Paper-white narcissus bulbs (enough to crowd the bowl)

1) Place a layer of gravel in the bowl. You can use pretty pebbles from the beach, or try aquarium gravel in different colors.

2) Add water up to the top of the gravel.

3) Set the bulbs, flat ends down, onto the gravel.

4) Place the bowl by a cool, sunny window. You'll have masses of fragrant flowers in four to six weeks!

UPKEEP: Keep the gravel wet.

Amazing Amaryllis

This flower makes a stunning holiday gift.

You will need:

> 1 4- to 6-inch clay pot
>
> *Potting soil*
>
> 1 *amaryllis bulb*

1) Fill the pot three-quarters of the way with soil.

2) Bury the bulb, allowing just the pointy end to stick above the soil.

3) Water and place in a sunny window.

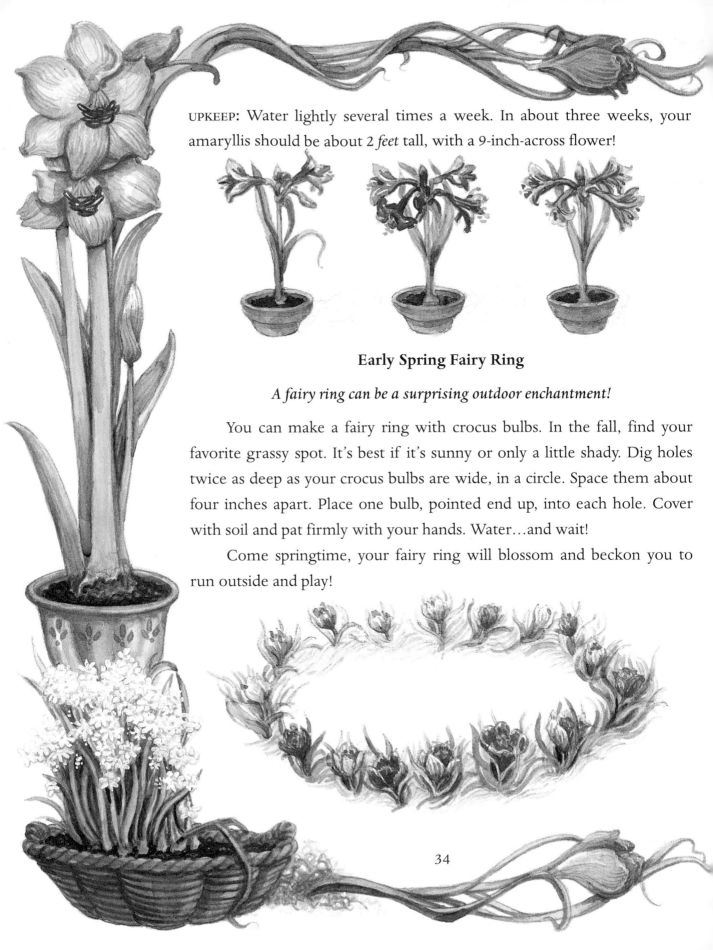

UPKEEP: Water lightly several times a week. In about three weeks, your amaryllis should be about 2 *feet* tall, with a 9-inch-across flower!

Early Spring Fairy Ring

A fairy ring can be a surprising outdoor enchantment!

You can make a fairy ring with crocus bulbs. In the fall, find your favorite grassy spot. It's best if it's sunny or only a little shady. Dig holes twice as deep as your crocus bulbs are wide, in a circle. Space them about four inches apart. Place one bulb, pointed end up, into each hole. Cover with soil and pat firmly with your hands. Water...and wait!

Come springtime, your fairy ring will blossom and beckon you to run outside and play!

FRIENDSHIP GARDEN

*Take a friend a snippet of one of your plants and ask if you
can have a snippet of one of hers. These pieces are called "cuttings."
With cuttings, you can create a garden in which each plant will
remind you of a favorite person or place!*

You can take cuttings from houseplants year-round. Cuttings from outdoor plants should be taken in the spring. To take a cutting, use clean scissors. Snip several inches off the tip of a healthy, leafy plant. Take off all the leaves except the few top ones. With an adult's help, dust the stem with "rooting hormone," a product available at most garden centers. Rooting hormone isn't absolutely necessary, but it does help!

Fill a small container with potting soil. With a straight twig make a hole several inches deep. Insert the stem of your cutting into the hole. Only the little leafy top should show. Press the cutting gently in place, and water with a spray bottle until it's completely damp.

Cuttings need to be kept warm and protected. A window sill over a radiator is an ideal spot for a cutting, but on top of a refrigerator often works nicely, too. Check newly potted cuttings daily to make sure the soil around them is moist. Water cuttings with a fine mist from a spray bottle. Be careful not to let them dry out.

MAKING SCENTS

Lavender's blue, dilly, dilly, lavender's green.
When I am king, dilly, dilly, you shall be queen.

The easiest way to stir your imagination, revive memories, and lift your spirits is to breathe in a delicious smell. Lavender and sage are wonderfully aromatic herbs that are easy to grow and will return to your garden bigger and better each year.

Lavender and Sage

Lavender and sage require full sun and average soil with good drainage. Transplants are available at most garden centers. Buy them in the spring, after all danger of frost is past. They can be transplanted into your garden or into a container.

To harvest lavender flowers, cut off the long spikes at the top of the plants just as the purple buds on the tips begin to open. Pick sage leaves and stems throughout the summer growing season, as you need them. Make sure you harvest a big batch before the first frost.

Many container-grown herbs will not survive outside during the winter. Bring them inside and water them carefully so they do not dry out. If your herbs are in the garden, cut them back an inch or two from the ground in the fall.

Lavender Wand

You will need:

25 fresh, long lavender spikes
2 strong rubber bands

1) Remove any leaves from the spikes.

2) Tightly wrap a rubber band around the bunch, just below the flower heads.

3) Hold the bunch upside down, with the *flowers* in one fist.

4) Bend the stems down to one side over your fist.

5) Grasp the bottom of the stems with your other hand.

6) Carefully let go of the flower heads and wrap another rubber band tightly around the stems.

7) Arrange the stems so they form a little cage around the flowers.

8) Cover the last rubber band with a pretty ribbon, and trim the stems with scissors.

9) Tuck the wand into a drawer for sweet-smelling clothes.

Herbal Bath Powder

For this delicious herb-scented powder, you can either buy ground sage or grind your own. Put 1 tablespoon of ground sage, 1 tablespoon of store-bought ground cloves, and 3 tablespoons of cornstarch into a plastic container with a tight-fitting lid. Put the lid on tightly and shake the container to mix the powder. Now sprinkle a little powder on yourself to smell as fresh as a garden!

Spice Up Your Life

❧ Hang a bunch of dried lavender in your closet.

❧ Dry leafy sage branches and twist them into a fragrant wreath.

❧ Add fresh sage to scrambled eggs or omelets.

❧ Make a lavender sachet by tying a handful of dried lavender into a handkerchief with a pretty ribbon.